# 7 STEPS TO MAKING YOUR FIRST APP

*THESE 7 MONEY-MAKING TIPS WILL SAVE YOU TIME AND ENERGY*

### SUSANNE BIRGERSDOTTER

# Introduction

*THANK YOU* for downloading this e-book.

I recently had the good fortune to meet the fashion designer Calvin Klein. I listened as he talked about his way of always thinking of the future, planning ahead and realizing his vision for his business.

Calvin Klein's keynote talk made me refocus my business plans: I would forget about the past and base my future business decisions on my current situation. The world today is moving so rapidly that in order to make the right decisions, you need to focus on short production runs, evaluate the results, and then choose the next direction. Be flexible and kill your darlings. If you can stay ahead of your competitor, that's great, but also bear in mind that there is space for more than one player, and being first is not always the best. Having the knowledge of who is first and where you are in the market, however, is vital. And keep in mind that staying ahead at all times will keep you in the top spot in your industry.

The past 5 years were both my heaven and my hell. I chose to step out of my comfort zone and into a kick-ass zone. I developed several new companies in 4 years. I met new friends, I almost went bankrupt, lost all my money and took a leap of faith, facing the insecurity of running my own business, taking on responsibility for paying others' salaries while keeping none of the revenue for myself for months.

I wanted to do something, create something – to become an entrepreneur and business leader. In order to do achieve those goals, I had to find my inner strength and take a huge jump into the unknown.

It was not easy. I was in new, difficult territory, and I really didn't know what it was that I wanted to do. I just knew it wasn't what I had been doing. Then one day, my daughter came home and was having a hard time learning her multiplication tables. I looked on my iPad for an app for this specific purpose but found nothing that I could use. Realizing that there was a need for this kind of app, I googled "How to make your own app," and the rest, as they say, is history.

After two days of research I knew enough to develop my own app for the multiplication tables, and after three months, I had the app available in different languages for children all over the world.

Almost everyone depends on apps, and there is a huge, and growing, market for apps worldwide. Knowing this, I went from having one app to 20 apps, all in the space of eight months.

I saw the potential for having an entire business centred on apps. I continued to work with people online to create more apps. I did not know how to code or develop, so I created a team around me to do those tasks, and we reached the Top 10 in sales, and even in a short space of time, amazingly moving into #1 spot in the Apple App Store. It was possible to build such a business, and I was apparently good at it!

Plan for the future and trust your gut! That is what I did, and now I have reached a point where I am confident that anything can be done.

Don't let anything hold you back. Just decide to do it, then go for it. If someone else has done it, why shouldn't you? I am living proof of the potential to succeed. And even though I received bad family-related news during the time when I was setting up my business, and even though I lost money – a lot of money – I still forged ahead and came out on top. Like planning to have children, the time is never really "right" – you just have to go for it!

These are my tips for making your own app and for getting out of your comfort zone and into your kick-ass zone. In sharing these tips with you, I am also proving to myself that I am a brave a woman with inner-strength and the ability to become whatever I want to become. I also hope to show that the journey to self-awareness is worth anything. It is about continuing to grow as a person.

As crazy as it might seem, the apps I had initially developed successfully were rather small projects. When I was starting out, they seemed huge! Now, as I have found my way into this crazy business, my head spins thinking about the enormous gap between where I started out and the success I have today.

After the multiplication app, a location app, the diet #1 app and a few other innovative apps that helped to place us on the map as an app business, I wanted to produce a huge hit: something that would be noticed. Really noticed.

We have looked at many different options and realized that the most successful apps were gaming apps, and we found a gap in the market. This was in 2014, and there were only a handful of location-based games on the market, all of which were of very poor quality. It felt that the opportunity was simply laying there waiting for us, and I decided to start creating what had a chance to become **the** biggest handheld game in the world. Why think small when big is available, right? But this venture needed more capital than my small app company had at the time. I needed to get investors on board, and this task brought an interesting new chapter in my life: tackling the venture capital market and raising capital. Could I do it?

Even though that market was complex and needed in-depth investigation, I started a gaming company to get going, and indeed I succeeded. But this is a story I will tell you all about in another publication.

This book is about how I made my first app in 2012, what I have learnt since then, and how you can follow in my steps.

# THIS IS HOW I MADE MY FIRST APPS.

*As I usually say, if you know something, then it's easy. But if you don't know it, even the simplest things can be hard.*

Those of you who have built apps or websites/web software may find a lot of this text to be very basic, and maybe you do things another way. But I struggled through the app development process with no prior tech experience, using trial and error and, in trying to keep costs down, doing most of the work myself. I did many things wrongly, but I embraced failure and learnt from my mistakes. *Every failure gives you more knowledge to go down the right path.*

Also, as you read, don't forget that I'm self-taught and that there might be common business practices out there that I don't follow. I focus on making apps for companies and people with dreams, using the lessons I learnt from my own experiences.

So read on, use what you want from the book and maybe I can give you some hints on how to make your first app.

---

*And as you know, it's all up to you.*

---

## BACKGROUND

As we move more and more into a digital world and people become more mobile, the demand and usage of apps that connect individuals with each other and with businesses and provide information and entertainment will grow exponentially.

This concept became a total game changer when Apple launched the iPhone. It allowed you access to apps that you could carry around with you everywhere and use anywhere. This knowledge alone can make you a specialist in market demand today. Don't forget that the first app makers out there were once where you are now: with the seed of an idea for the next step in your life.

Apps are so small and simple, whether they be utility apps or games. Everybody can relate to apps, whether you use them for entertainment, information, education, or just to connect with others - it's all there at your fingertips.

Although more complicated to create than a mobile website, they are much easier to use. This has opened up an opportunity for many people to get into business fairly easily, sometimes at low cost, and the app stores can display, distribute and sell the app to the world, in every market, no matter where in the world you live.

Apps can be translated into many different languages thereby opening up even more markets, enabling you to achieve even bigger success. You can of course choose to have your app in stores around the world in the same language, usually English, but then making available translations can make all the difference. Once it's done and available, then investigate further what can be improved, or what will appeal in a specific market - then create/develop another app and launch, distribute and sell it over and over again.  It's a commodity to be traded in many ways.

It's all up to you - and it CAN be done...

# WHY YOU SHOULD READ THIS BOOK

Many people realize today that apps are what drive mobile interactions and that they are becoming the medium for people to connect with each other, businesses and organizations. More and more people are going mobile each day, be it on their Smartphone or their other devices. We cannot get away from the fact that everyone is staying connected with each other worldwide. The app business will most certainly grow for years to come because it's easy, available and understandable for both customers and developers. That's the appeal: simple, easy and cheap. The simplicity of the app and smartphone is here to stay for the foreseeable future.

Developing and launching your own app can open a completely new world for your business and your life. Whatever happens, it is a product that you made, that is available for everyone to see and relate to, give feedback on and, if you did it well, use daily and give you praise.

This book will help you to debunk some of the myths around developing and launching your app, and it will also provide you with valuable insight into this ever-changing dynamic world. From providing you with valuable information about what you must consider, tips of what you should do and what to watch out for - this will become your go-to reference for the future.

# Table of Contents

## Step 1. You have an idea

So you have an idea for an app. I can tell you that EVERYBODY has an idea for an app today.

I meet people every day and pretty much everybody is talking about their great disruptive app idea. And the first question is: how much does it cost to make an app? And it's the answer to that question that I'm trying to give you in this book because as with many things, there are a lot of answers. Even when the idea is on the table, it's almost impossible to get an answer without some serious groundwork.

So before anything else you must first put pen to paper (yes, the old fashioned way, or any other way of viewing your work, of course) and map out what this idea is all about. It might sound strange but this is a good way to find out if your idea is good even to you. Talk is cheap, writing is real. If you can't explain it in writing you can't continue – that's that. Then, keep on thinking. I am sure that some of you, who will sit down with a pen, will have a problem to write down an elevator pitch of your app idea. Try it. However if you can then you should consider things like:

- Who is going to use this app?

- What is its purpose / what problem is it going to solve?

- What exactly do you want the app to do?

- How will it simplify somebody's life?

- How are you going to make it appeal to the users?

- What will make this different from other apps out there?

- Will people pay for what it does? Would you?

You must set your goal for this app and what you want to achieve with it, and then work from there.

If you do not already have an idea for an app, but would like to come up with one, either for your existing business or as a new business opportunity, the best way approach is to do your research on the app stores. See which types of apps are most popular, and then develop your idea from that. If you are lucky enough, you can find a gap in the market that is waiting for you to fill. Otherwise, you can go for improvement:

*Develop you app from what is already working out in the market and just make it better... People make so many apps so badly. Just package it better.*

## THE BASICS

There are so many apps out there, both good and bad that you want to make sure yours sticks, that your app stands out from the crowd and that it will have people coming back to it all the time and telling everybody else about it as well. If you are lucky enough, your app will go viral!

You need to *make your app easily accessible to all of the people you target,* make *people need or want to get back to the app*, and try to make it something the user will share with others.

That makes it possible to go viral, and that is obviously the best marketing you can get. Do not overcomplicate the app. Make it simple and easy to use. The more complex it gets, the more expensive it becomes when developing, and there is no surety that complex is better. In fact, going simple is usually better.

To be absolutely honest, you don't know what, exactly, will appeal to people. It's very interesting to find out how wrong one is when launching apps. Sometimes, the things you think will be most appealing are the least appealing, and vice versa. So if you are not a pro, and even if you are, try to release the MVP – "the minimum viable product" – so that you can see what directions and changes you have to make to get it just right.

Make your app fit a niche, and look for coming trends in that market segment and develop the app around that. A good way to try your first app is to use an interest that is close to you heart. That gives you first hand knowledge on what you as an experienced practitioner would like from the app. It's all about what you will get out of the app, how you get it, and how the user handles it. Say for example that you are an expert horse rider: What do horse riders need? Look at the market and what is currently available in app stores. Look what has already been done. Then, use your own skills to make an improvement, and go for it!

This background research also helps in promoting your app later, since you probably already have an existing market, regardless of how small.

Another way of looking for inspiration is to search online for what apps are really dominating the market and then see how you could model your app on what they are doing. Don't try and re-invent the wheel - just make it better.

**ACTION STEPS**

Do your research online, in the identified niches and in the app stores.

- If there are none similar, why? Because of luck or that you are the smartest on the planet?

- If there are many others, can you compete?

- Finalize your idea and then get to work

- Be critical of your own ideas.

- Don't reinvent the wheel.

## STEP 2. IT'S ALL IN THE DETAIL

This is where the magic starts happening, where things start getting real and we separate the not-so-good big-talkers from the hard-working wanting-this-more-than-anything entrepreneurs. This phase is also where you can really let your ideas take flight and then weed them out until only the most powerful, impactful ideas remain.

This is also where you have to decide if you want to do this yourself or if you are going to hand the work over to someone else. It's all about money. The work has to be done, and either you pay for it or do it yourself. The hard way or the easy way. In this book I will explain to you how you do it yourself. But if you are handing it over to someone else, you can learn some useful stuff and make some smart comments and ask the right questions on the process and their quote, if you read on.

It will be hard, but it's doable and doing it once will make it possible for you to do it again and again. I went for it myself.

It's at this stage where you *decide how complex your app must be or not be.* You need to write down, again on paper, exactly what it is you want. You are like a songwriter developing a number one song or a filmmaker doing the script and storyboard for your film. It's all in the detail, and it all has to be done.

Write down everything that you can think of that will make this app be a knockout success using your research and what has worked for others. This is where every button, touch, move, comma and detail counts. So be structured, thinking of what should be done at every step.

- For example, if there is a button what should it do?

If this is the first app you build, I suggest that you do an MVP. It's a minimum viable product, and don't overdo it. You can always come back and make more later, but now you just want to get it out there. Make it simple, get it out in the stores and test it. Then, you can make expansions.

I can't stress enough that the details are in the groundwork- so, here is a chapter you will need to really get things done.

## THE DETAILS

This can be done on paper and is how I started, but the tools available online are simple to use, cheap and give you the visual possibility to press and see the flow as well as getting a decent overview of the project and number of screens. This is the project's blueprint and the better it is, the better your price and time estimation will be.

So, use the tools, or pen and paper, make your first screen view, and you will immediately end up with some thoughts like: where is my artist; I need a picture, maybe a motion animation, or splash screen; which font should I use; and what colours look best. If you have the eye and/or you are a pro at Photoshop, you will have it easy. Otherwise, you need to get help, and this is the way to go through the whole process: trial and error, and evaluation of what you can do and what you can´t do.

Any way that you get the work done is good, but going step by step from a user perspective is my advice. You might want to change your method later, once you get the hang of things, but right now, it's the best way.

Get the splash screen and the logo out of the way either by an artist or by yourself.  If you want it to move then get ahold of an animator. If you want 3D, you need to find a 3D animator. (There are more job titles in this business than people in the shops on Black Friday, and you will need a lot of these people. It is therefore important to learn the tricks on how to find the right one and what sites are the best for people skills-searching)

It's also very likely there's an app or website that offers a simple version of what you need, so have a look. Using such tools, which are usually free (at least to start with), you can make a reasonable prototype or sketch to hand over to the professional. This will save you time and money and make it easier to obtain a cost estimate that will hold water.

These first pages should be nice looking, appealing and professional (all should be of course). The first pages normally go quite quickly in the process since they don't have so much functionality.

Next is probably log in, the most boring part of the app, but it has to be done: account recovery, joining with Facebook, etc. This is where you start to see the complexity. Should users log in with email or get a username? (*Personally, I hate usernames and prefer to use only email as logins.*) Should the account be confirmed by email, or should they get the password to their email? Decisions, decisions – and you have to take them on. Just do it!

---

*At the beginning it's amazing how many questions can arise, and this is only the start.*

---

## DECISIONS, DECISIONS....

The more groundwork you get done now, the more you will save time and money and more likely you are to get what you asked for.

I must also warn you that most apps have a view from several perspectives. By that, I mean that if you do something it is seen in one way by the current user and another by others, and sometimes there are more people involved. Keep the flows in order and make sure you have a screen for all the views clearly stated. I try to use different colour scheming to keep track of different perspectives.

When you have decided on the login procedure, then you should get on with the actual app behaviour. What choices are there on this screen, the menu? How many options and buttons? And again, the design. Look at other apps for design options. What do you like, what fits with what, and who is your target audience?

You want people to get to the core action as soon as possible. Should they be able test the functionality before going live with the app, and how will they know what to do? Is it intuitive enough? Will they know what to do when they see the page, or do you need help texts?

Put the button "start" as a first. What should happen? When that is pressed, what should happen? Take out a new piece of paper and draw what will happen. Draw a "back"- button in the top corner. Maybe a menu burger in the corner so that you can always open a menu for options, but there are many options so have a look at other apps – or just go crazy creative!

Now you are well on your way! Continue like this and place all pages with screens for each action and button. Write explanations and flows on how things work.

Again, the clarity and thoroughness of this is what makes all the difference for the developers in the end, and doing it well will make it cheaper and save time.

Now when all the pages are done it's easier to get a decent price and time for the app development, as well as set a timeline for production. You will begin to see if the app is still going to be that amazing idea that you had in the beginning.

An app idea can be fairly abstract, but now you can see your idea almost realized. You can decide if the idea will hold water or not. And you should now show and explain to someone on the flows and handling of your app idea. If this now still seems like a good idea, then just go for it. You might actually have a success on your hands.

This screen overview that you have now drawn is your blueprint and is essential to the continuation of the project, just like the storyboard for a movie.

*SCREEN OVERVIEW AND WHY IT IS NECESSARY*

A screen overview is nothing more than a glorified storyboard. This is where you take your sketches that you have made, translate them digitally and it gives your idea more clarity and functionality.

This will become **the foundation to your app development** and is a crucial step in the process. You can do this yourself with tools like Weld or FluidUi.

But I want to emphasize that there are no corners to cut here: it is a time consuming job, and it must be thought through and presented well.

With this screen overview, you can now get a whole lot of information that you will need to be able to proceed. You must know what the app is all about so that you can decide on what people will be involved.

- Artist to make the design, PSDs and slicing

- Backend/ server programmer for communication between apps

- Android developer for Android

- IOS developer. For iPhone

There are pros and cons with having more people. One person requires less contact but makes the project longer. The developers are rarely as good as they say on everything; they have their specialties, and at the end of the day it's all about time. If you already have decided to pay, then it might be good to pay three people for a third of the time rather than one person who will take three times as long.

# Step 3. The technical stuff

In the previous step it was all about you and your vision, what you see for your app. It was all developed on paper and now it becomes more tangible.

In this next step, it gets more practical and the vision now becomes real. It's about filling in the gaps, it's about determining and allocating the tasks that need to be performed and finding the right people, the right platform and taking action.

### Let's be specific

When your Screen Overview is done you need to write down a list of actions. Let's call this list a technical specification.

That actions listed in the technical specification describe what is happening on each page. This will be a piece of cake when you have a good Screen Overview. And this list is to give the programmers a good start by showing what all the buttons and actions are planned to do so they can program them properly.

- Didn't I tell you it would be time-consuming?

- And that you should cut it down to a minimum viable product?

- You probably have cut away some things already.

A professional programmer can now see what obstacles might be ahead and tell you what you need in terms of expertise or programming. The programmer can now give you a delivery date and quote that are realistic.

These are some of the things that you will need to look at in this step. Depending on your app, there may be more factors to consider, but probably not less. If you do not have the tech knowledge to speak to these people, then find somebody who does and make them part of your team. You cannot afford for your vision to fall flat here, just because of a miscommunication or lack of expertise. If you ask from a user perspective, clearly articulate what you want and expect to get, you will go quite far.

- Front End - is the part done in the phones, iOS or Android? Do you need both?

- Back End = Server. Does your app require server connection due to communication, saving, login procedure? Some things can be done through the app stores, like leader boards and other things. A local app, only in the phone with no server connection is the easiest to make. An App like the "2048" for example, can be done in 24 hours, by a reasonable programmer.

- Cross platform.  This is a good idea in some cases. In theory it's a way of programming the apps to an extent as one and then publishing them easily on all platforms. My experience is that when it comes to games the engines are great and necessary, but with less complicated apps then you should go for programming native, for each platform. It will give you less headaches.

- The screen overview and technical specification - are they good enough for the team? Very likely they will say yes. Planning is not one of their best efforts.

Take your time, and go through everything in detail to get any questions down on paper for later use.

## ART TECHNICAL

When it comes to design there are a lot of titles again. But what you need is every page/screen done in a PSD (photo shop layers) so you have all the layers and the work in a reusable way if you need to change or add artwork at a later date. You will have paid for this design, so you should have it in its raw format. That goes just as well for the source code. The PSDs are the source code of art. Then this PSD has to be sliced into each different asset to .png format. Slicing is to take each movable part and save it in a loose format so that it can be individually used by the programmers.

And this has to be done for each screen resolution and size for each device. It can look like this:

- iOS iPhone: @3x, @2x, @1x

- iOSiPad @2x,@1x

- Android Sizes XXXHDPI, XXHDPI, XHDPI, HDPI, MDPI

Make sure you get this into the art agreement because this is necessary, and everybody dislikes it, even the designer.

You hear? The job title doesn't even appeal: Slicer!

## THE PEOPLE

Working with people you don't know around the world requires patience and cleverness. Even working in your hometown with people you can actually meet will have its problems, so just imagine what happens working with someone you can't reach. What if they are someone you can never get hold of or fight in court if needed?

So this is a delicate problem. However, in the new digital economy, there are many great people out there who will do their utmost to do a good job. You just have to find out who they are. Try to find samples of their work. Always get them to talk to you face to face at least once. There are more and more people who claim to be who and what they are not.

Make sure you have leverage, and that leverage is very likely monetary. Paying before delivery is a big risk and must be limited. The payment should be results-based. So what result did you agree on?

In larger projects where payments are done on a results basis, you will end up with the problem that you have more to lose at one point, and that always occurs when the project starts to become a bit more complicated. When the developers might realize they have bitten off more than they can chew and can't really deliver. It doesn't always occur, but it sometimes happens that they might consider leaving the project and be content with the money paid so far. <u>But you will have nothing</u>.

Don't forget that if you are not a coder, this person has a great advantage: the knowledge of the code. Code can be very clear, but it can also be an impenetrable rat nest. On more than one occasion, I have had to throw away completed work and start over. Documentation of the code is often the key, and most programmers don't mind doing it – they might even take pride that their code is tidy and documented. But that requires time, and at the end of the day if you push them, that's the first thing that is going to go out the window. Documentation may seem unnecessary now, but it might mean everything later down the road. Coders could get ill, leave for other jobs, or break their arms. When it comes to code, every code is very individualized. Since you cannot read code and have no idea, you are in the coders' hands.

And since the app stores, standards and phones keep changing and being improved or updated, you must also be able to *update your app regularly*. Build a great relationship with your programmer so that this never becomes a problem. Coding is very personal, and changing to a new programmer can be disastrous. Well, at least it very often requires a fresh start.

But again, I must say that if it comes to that and you fall out with your programmer, make the best out of it. It is what it is, and now you have learnt the lesson and won't repeat it again.

At least you know what you must not do next time!

## Step 4. Don't forget about the contracts

As with anything in business, especially if it involves services performed and money, there **needs to be a valid contract**. Contracts need to be stipulated upfront, and you need to ensure that **everybody fully understands and agrees** to what is contained in the contract. Before anything is enacted, a contract must be drafted, discussed, amended if needed, and then signed, with copies provided to everybody concerned. This is to make sure that there will be no misunderstandings or disputes in the future that end up in legal battles, costing everybody involved huge amounts of money.

Before heading off, however, and appointing an attorney to set up a complex contract that is going to cost you quite a bit of money, first look at exactly how you want to protect yourself and the service provider that you will be using. In many cases a Memorandum of Understanding will suffice and a formal contract may be an over kill.

Let's just define exactly what each of these is:

### DEFINITION OF A CONTRACT

This is an agreement creating obligations enforceable by law.

The basic elements of a contract are mutual assent, consideration, capacity, and legality. In some jurisdictions, the element of consideration can be satisfied by a valid substitute.

### DEFINITION OF A MEMORANDUM OF UNDERSTANDING

This is a formal agreement between two or more parties.

Companies and organizations can use MOUs to establish official partnerships. MOUs are not legally binding but they carry a degree of seriousness and mutual respect, stronger than a gentlemen's agreement (**note** that a MOU may be legally binding if it satisfies all of the six elements of a contract).

Before you can decide which of these two would be the best option for you, there are some things that you first need to decide. Also take into consideration that you will not have one legal document that will cover all service providers - each one will need to have their own.

## THE AGREEMENT - WHAT SHOULD BE INCLUDED AT MINIMUM

Before setting up the agreement you must have clarity on *what the project is all about, what your end-goals are and how the services required are to be performed.*

Write it down in your own words- what is your desired result, your goal and vision for the end product. Things like your screen overview and technical specifications also need to be included in the agreement and will ensure a better result.

You might also need to decide *how this agreement will be signed* - what are the rules, especially if you are dealing with service providers worldwide. *Legal rules may differ between countries*, so this must also be taken into consideration.

All participants to the agreement must be vetted up front and checks done regularly if the contract duration is for an extended period.

If you, for some reason, cannot get into a legal dispute with a person, whether it's because of the financial situation of you or the programmer, the distance between you, or other reasons for which legal action would not be realistic, the need for a proper contract might not be necessary. It's all up to the people with whom you're working. However, ownership, deliveries and costs should always be covered in as much detail as possible. Again I must stress that you should get everything on paper. People understand differently. THEY DO!

Make sure that the *language being used is understood by all,* especially when dealing with foreign service providers.

Some basic points that should always be included:

Project start and end dates

Milestones should be clearly defined

Include a penalty clause with clear conditions of what is covered

Include a confidentiality clause

Be as detailed as possible in your scope of work

Source codes need to be accessible and fully delivered to you.

Include a clause that stipulated that IP - Intellectual Property - remains yours

Include clause about verification and testing of software

Include a clause about updates and changes

Clearly define the roles and responsibilities of all parties and their channels of communication

Include a clause to ensure that any art is original art and is royalty, trademark and copyright free.

Any issues around licensing, specifically third party licensing, needs to be defined and highlighted in the agreement

Include a breach clause, listing any and instances that would result in a breach of the agreement

Specify project cost, as well as how and when the service provider will be paid and what the conditions for payment will entail

Last but not least, *all parties must get a signed copy of the agreement* sent to them either via email or a physical copy, as they stipulate, to ensure that at no point can somebody turn around and say they never received a copy or do not know what is contained within the agreement.

## STEP 5. IT'S SHOW-TIME - GETTING THE WORK DONE

Now stuff gets real. The *screen overview is available*. The *technical specs have been created*; you *have the assets and the art as well as a contract signed by all*. Now you can get to work. If everything mentioned *above is not in place*, my advice is that ***YOU DO NOT START development***.

Essentially, you have created your team, and they are only now ready to really get moving. Your milestones (both major and minor) are the main drivers of the project, so make sure that they are communicated to all and that everybody knows exactly to what point you have progressed.

This is trickier than it seems since this is your baby, and you will climb mountains to reach the top. Your team, however, sees the project as a form of income, a job, or the next task in line, one of many, so make sure to not make the mistake of treating your team as if they share equally in your drive for success. Do they want to work weekends just because you want to?

### GETTING HOLD OF THE PEOPLE

To be able even to try to make an app, you needed a programmer. So that was something of a prerequisite for the whole project, and it was the knowledge of that market that triggered me to even start with making an app for my daughter.

### THE ONLINE WORK PLACES

Smart Internet entrepreneurs realized years ago that there would be a demand for buying and selling skills online. Producing code, managing social media, blogging, copywriting – pretty much anything can be traded indefinitely online. Anyone with a skill to offer professionally could demonstrate their abilities and get hired online. A huge market has evolved, and discovering the market is what made my success possible in the first place. If I hadn't known then - the thought of creating an app without any app skills would have never surfaced at all. So lucky me!

I did it with companies called Upwork.com and Fiverr.com but there are many options out there. Just look around online and use the one you like best.

As I have said before, it is not an easy task to find the right people so take it easy, and be sure of their ability to deliver before starting to pay and trust them. They may or may not be good developers. One popular move is to have a very nice female picture and then refuse to talk to you. They turn out to be middle-aged men. Starting out with a lie is not a great sign.

The companies I mentioned have great ways of securing transactions, at least to some extent, which serves to minimize the problems that can occur.

### MANAGEMENT TOOL/S

As there are quite a number of service providers taking part in this project, *a management tool to co-ordinate all the tasks and responsibilities* of everybody is key to the success of the project.

*Assembla.com* is a good online tool to use for this type of project. Loved by programmers and pretty much hated by creative souls, it allows you to manage your milestones as well as keeping everybody in contact. Having access to tickets in the system makes everything much simpler from a track and trace point of view, as tasks are assigned via a ticket system and tracked to completion. There are many similar apps / programs available to manage projects of this nature, so it is best that you find the one that suits you and your team perfectly.

Skype and email are the backup type tools for alternative irregular type communication. Form groups in Skype to ensure that everybody gets access to or copies of the various communications.

Key to the usage of one of these programs is a repository where source code can be kept etc. Make sure that the one you choose has such functionality.

Make sure that all material is constantly updated and sent to one place, for instance drop box. Even if it's a small project it will be a lot of material and it's not advised to have it spread out everywhere.

The frequency of feedback from the team needs to be determined at the beginning of the project and then adhered to with no excuses, be it weekly, fortnightly or monthly - the project owner needs to decide what would be best after discussion with the team.

Communication is key and there for you need to keep it tight. Put your foot down as soon as you find something that starts to not go according to your plan. If you are spread around the globe, there might be millions of excuses, and I have heard them all – from earthquakes, to family deaths, to festivals, to storms, to power failures, to all kind of family matters – but they only get worse if you don't stop it from the start. (The earthquake, however, was actually the truth and not a recurring event!)

A good plan is to have the developers send you a daily report summarizing what they have done and what they will do tomorrow and refer to screens, technical specs or tickets. That will keep you up to date, and you are more or less sure of the progress.

This takes some time, but it's never a problem if they are pros and not happy amateurs trying to make a buck.

When choosing people, make sure you can work in the same time zone. It might be frustrating to start when they finish; you need some time together to straighten out the question marks. And trust me, there will be question marks. This can be very frustrating in many ways, and don't be surprised if your Skype notification starts to go berserk in the middle of the night when your developer starts asking questions when starting their day on the other side of the planet. That is good news but can become a problem with your partner, who might not like it as much.

These worksites try to keep the seller and buyer in the system. This is because they need to earn their money in the transaction, which is all well and good. This however means that they try to keep communication inside the confinements of the site and that is a problem since their tools are not always exactly as smooth as the big ones.

You will need to get hold of people at times for different reasons and there is no reason to not give out a mobile phone number or let them Face-time you, if it is a serious service provider. However, if they do not want to do it, this should raise a red flag that there is something shady going on.

And regarding worksites, I suggest you keep the actual transactions within their system, since that gives you an extra security if there should be any problems with the delivery. At least you can get them banned. These sites also have a possibility to freeze money in case of a dispute and some even have insurances included for certain developers.

Things to watch out for:

> Profiles with women profile pictures that don't want to talk to you.

> People that don't want to communicate outside the worksites with the personal phones and devices.

> Communication is everything when it comes to this kind of hiring. Any kind of glitch in how you want to communicate is a bad sign and should be considered right away. (It will very likely not change for the better!)

> People who claim they can do anything. No one is an expert in every code language. Watch out.

If all their prior work is confidential due to the customers. Ask for similar work from previous jobs so you can compare.

Aggressive behaviour should just not be accepted you should NOT have to explain why they are not the ones you hire.

Different cultures can be confusing. Make sure you stick with the ones you can manage well.

# Step 6. Launching to the stores

Whilst the team is working hard to get the app ready, you should be working behind the scenes to get the app launched with a bang into the market.

Depending on the platform, you should already have *concluded contracts with either the Google Play or iTunes store.*

If you are working with the Apple iTunes stores, you should have a developer account set up and an iTunes connect account. A developer account can take several weeks before it is approved and available, so get it done early.

As with any other contracts, in both cases there is a substantial amount of "paperwork" that needs to be completed, so get it done and submitted as quickly as you can - *it can take a number of weeks before everything is approved* and you have access to the consoles.

The idea with these app stores is to make things as simple as possible for you as the owner and developer of the app. For use of this facility, they take 30% of your profits but they handle pretty much everything for you in return.

All you need to do is determine your pricing strategy and put the relevant price on your app, which you can change any time you like. The best thing is to read and become familiar with the store's rules and then stick to those rules.

Payment will be made to you 2 months after the actual sale of the app to the user.

Another added benefit of using the app stores is that they market your app for you and manage the whole process, in addition to providing you with hundreds of different tools to show you how your app is performing.

However, the app stores get hundreds of new entries every day and the top performing apps you see tend to be limited to a few lucky (hard working and / or rich) ones. So you are left to people searching for your app or finding it through advertising or editorials - pretty much like any tangible product in actual stores.

It is hard work to get to the top shelf. Really hard work, so use any means available to you.

INSIDE THE APP STORES

Make full use of the functionality and tools that are provided inside the app stores. There are a number of hints and tips, and useful step-by-step guides to create the best possible presentation.

One critical thing is to make sure that you provide good content and clear, attention-grabbing images. You want to make sure that whoever is searching for an app like yours finds *your* app in the store.

This will only happen if you make sure that your copy/content is targeted to your intended audience and describes your app in detail, including, most importantly, what benefits it will provide the potential customer.

Google should release your app in about two days but it can take longer.

Apple has a more in-depth review of your app, and their release program will take longer. They will also take the time to test the app to make sure everything works, so PLEASE test everything BEFORE submitting it to any of the stores. Although Apple have stated that the period has decreased, it can take up to 2 weeks from launch to until it appears in the store, and you can get rejected if it's not good enough and then you end up last in line again, and it's another two weeks and that can go on.

Now, when you are in the stores is when you understand that viral is good. It's when a person likes what you have done and shares it online with one or more friends. You should therefore add ways of sharing in your app. If it offers scores, images, or lists, encouraging social media sharing of these things is a good way to try to go viral. You never know – you might be the next big thing just because it is the right timing, like the Flappy birds effect.

### ADVERTISING

Before launching, even during the production phase of your app, start to consider optional ideas for how you can monetize your app. Besides charging for the app, you could look at providing advertising space in your app, including things like banners and videos.

Monetizing is a skill. After your hard work you would probably like to make some money. Of course, being at number 598 on the list in the store doesn't really pay the bills, so you will have to take some action. To get some traction you want to market your app with whatever means possible. This is of course an on going project. If the app is not taken care of, it will die, like a Tamagotchi.

# Step 7. Marketing your app

A lot of time and effort (and money) has gone into developing your app - why then would you throw it all away by not promoting it?

This is in many cases where the app falls flat, not due to poor design or bad interfaces, but because *nobody is aware of it.* Whether the app is your business or you have developed an app for your business - as its creator, you need to *get the message out to the marketplace* that it is available

In many cases the creator of the app does not have a huge marketing budget available to spend on getting the message out there, but even if you do, poor marketing will amount to nothing.

Here are some creative ways to market your app that will not break the bank and in many cases will even go a very long way in building your credibility and brand at the same time.

## 8 WAYS TO CREATIVELY MARKET / PROMOTE YOUR APP

### CONNECT WITH CURRENT CUSTOMERS

Most of us forget to reach out to the customers we already have. These individuals already like and trust us, so why not get them on board before your design has been finalized and use their input and feedback to further improve your app. By asking for their input, you may discover gaps that will make this app skyrocket to #1.

### REACH OUT TO INFLUENCERS IN THE INDUSTRY OR IN THE SPECIFIC NICHE

Work on developing, honest, authentic and mutually beneficial relationships with influencers in the industry or niche. Then when your app is ready and you have added value for them, they will feel obliged to return the favour. Having access to their followers to promote your app will raise your app into the next level.

*CREATE A DEMO VIDEO*
Most individuals respond more favourably to images or video than any other means of communication. Showcasing exactly what your app is capable of and the value it can add into the life of the user makes it a very powerful marketing tool.

*BUILD YOUR APP ITS OWN LANDING PAGE*
Setting up a landing page for your app is like you have a super effective business card for yourself. You can fully demonstrate the functions and benefits of using the app, all in

living colour. In addition, you can include an effective call to action in almost every panel, multiplying out the power of the promotion exponentially.

*GET YOUR APP REVIEWED ON MOBILE APP SITES*
Mobile app sites get many more visitors than normal websites. When your pitch to the site is accepted and they review your app, you get exposure to their database of followers that normally measure in the tens of thousands. What better way to get the message out into the marketplace?

*PUT A LINK IN YOUR EMAIL SIGNATURE*
This might be one of the simplest, most effective ways of getting the message out there. As a business owner, just think of how many emails you send daily and if you have employees, get them to add the link in their signatures as well.

### CONNECT WITH LOCAL CUSTOMERS

Many of us attend local business networking sessions or Meet-ups in our area. Take along enough business cards that feature the download link for the app and hand out as many as you can to interested parties. For those people that are interested, please ask them to give you feedback after they have tested the app themselves.

### INNOVATE AND IMPROVE YOUR APP CONSTANTLY

In this fast paced environment, to stay ahead of the pack and your competition, be constantly updating the app and improving it for the benefit of the user. This will go a very long way in getting it shared with many more users or the message being shared about the kick-ass app you have developed.

There are many more ways to **market your app**, the key is to put yourself in the shoes of your user and decide where you will find them hanging out. ***Structure each marketing message*** as if you were talking directly to them, and ***build a connection with your target market.***

When the connection has been made, they will become the ambassadors for your app and your brand going forward.

## IN CLOSING

My advice on the way to success:

Maybe one of the most important steps is *not* about app development but about courage, about how to take the jump and believe in you dreams. If someone else can do it you can too!

In taking the leap, you will inevitably fail – and that's a great advantage if you have come to terms on **how to fail your way to Success!**

I could write a chapter on this theme alone, but time ticks regardless, and you can either make it worth something or just sit there and let it pass by. My experience has been filled with failures, laughter, successes and tears, and I made each of them count.

EVERYTHING IS POSSIBLE. BUT DON'T GET STUCK ON ONE THING. THAT WILL STOP YOU.

- Rethink the way to the goal; there is always another way

- Take smaller steps if necessary

- One small step is better than none.

- Try to take one step closer to goal at a day at least.

- Start with looking at yourself. Would you want it? Then consider your friends – would they pay for it?

FAILURE IS A PART OF SUCCESS. ALLOW YOURSELF TO FAIL.

- If you have not failed you have not tried hard enough.

- See clearly, limit failure

- Everything in your life, failure or success, is experience that makes us valuable.

- The more experience the more valuable.

- Try to not repeat failure

BECOME A SECRET AGENT. SPY ON YOUR COMPETITION (IF YOU HAVE ANY)

- More information is better

- Use tech

- Test and keep up

- Rethink and use, but wisely

Good luck, and love to you all, and thanks for reading this far.

If you like my incoherent babble then you should follow me in social media on FACEBOOK, TWITTER and INSTAGRAM

## About The Author

**Susanne Birgersdotter** is the founder and CEO of an independent group of global companies that create and develop digitial solutions with a disruptive edge. She is a sought-after international speaker and coach, and works as both an investor and mentor to others wanting to succeed in the start-up world.

Susanne's first company began with an idea at her kitchen table. She has a true entrepreneurial spirit and a passion for inspiring others to start their own "kitchen table" companies.

Today, she is in demand around the world as a female founder in a male-dominated industry. However, she sees this only as an advantage, as it makes her more motivated and determined to succeed. Susanne's goal is grow her companies, and at the same time inspire others to take the plunge into the entrepreneurial sphere.

Check her out on

www.sbdm.se

www.sthlmapplab.com

www.susannelive.com